ONE WITH GOD
The Power of Worship

By:

EWULOTAN AYODEJI PETER

All scriptures are from the King James Version of the Bible,
except otherwise stated

ISBN: 978-978-2261-22-9

ARTVIEW CREATIONS

Published & Printed in Nigeria

by Email: artviewc@gmail.com
Tel: +234-7049379624

Table of Content

DEDICATION

This book is dedicated to God Almighty Jehovah Elohim.

The one true God, the God Almighty, all-knowing God.

To my father and mother who brought me to this world. Late Apostle and Deconess, Festus and Oludoyinsola Ewulotanof The Apostolic Church. Though you couldn't wait to see me becoming a Pastor you want me to be.

Also to my mentor and father in the Lord. Late Rev. Dr. Francis Bola Akin-John. President, International Church growth ministry. For your fatherly care while on earth. Rest in peace dear father.

AKNOWLEDGEMENT

All thanks to God Almighty for the grace and divine inspiration to write this book. It has been the help of God and the inspiration of the Holy Spirit.

I also want to appreciate all inspiring authors who have written different inspiring and motivating topics on worship, praise with through encounter with God.

My gratitude also goes to my mentor and father in the Lord Late Rev. Francis Bola Akin-John for your sold out believe in me, your push, encouragement, nurturing me with words of God. You are a true father.

My profound appreciation also goes to my friend and brother, my personal person, Pastor Sunday Ogunade. My 360degree friend. Thanks for the push, encouragement and all the supports.

It will be out of sight if I fail to appreciate all SWITCH-TUNES for your commitment and believe in the switch-to worship ministry is at this time that the word worship, intimacy, Spirit etc become open up to me.

Thanks to my editor Mr Abiodun Mabadeje and Miss Oluwatosin Atolagbe (TeaShine). I appreciate all your inputs, your scarifies and commitment. My twin brother Pastor Dolapo Olowu thank you for not giving up. Distance is never a barrier between us. It seem we see everyday.

Special thanks to all member of Elohim Family Sanctuary

To my wife and one and only. Thank you for allowing me to serve God. Thank you for your support from day one of our friendship. Also a ig thank you to our children for being part of the story.

God bless you all.

INTRODUCTION

I some years back I have a concerns in ways by which believers life and walk with Jesus.

I began to ponder on worship, the music, the sound, the songs the ambience for worship, the lighting, the shouting and many money.

I had so many experience talk with God and asking questions. Reading books on worship and creating atmosphere worship.

In all my finding, began to understand that our ministry to the Lord is more than the song, the music, the shout, the lighting, the stage. Is our worship that make the difference. Our style of living, our heart, connection with God. It doesn't matter if you can sing or not, it doesn't matter the crowd or the stage.

Our worship is who we are and how we connect to our father that determine the freshness of all those other aspects of our walk with God.

This book will introduce you to different aspect of worship and we will see that your worship aid your life and give you a worthy experience of one and one with God.

CHAPTER 1: WHAT IS WORSHIP?

Worship is the expression of our love for God, stemming from who He is, what He has said, and His ongoing work in our lives. It encompasses more than just the music played during a church service; it's the totality of our service to God. Worship should be our primary purpose in life, and it's not limited to specific times or activities.

According to 1 Corinthians 10:31, everything we do should be done for the glory of God.

Webster's Dictionary defines worship as "to honor with extravagant love and extreme submission,"

As human being we are fashion to worship anything. Image, Spirit, to regard with great or extravagant respect, honor, or devotion. a celebrity worshiped by her fans. A farmer or hunter worship his cutlass or iron as god.

Oxford dictionary define worship as the practice of showing respect for God or a god, by saying prayers, singing with others,

Etymology. The word is derived from the Old English weorþscipe, meaning "worship, honour shown to an object", which has been etymologised as "worthiness" or "worth-ship" – in the sense of giving, at its simplest, value to something.

Man is a worshiper. Whether they acknowledge it or not, everybody worship. Some people worship their job, money, possession. Some worship TV star, music legend. Some worship there goal or desire, pleasure and some of us worship God of heaven and earth.

Understanding the meaning of worship will help us to have a shift in positioning our mind and getting our priority right.

The essential idea is that whatever it is that you value most highly or place the greatest worth upon is what you worship. So we see that people worship many things, but the truth is worship rightfully belong to God, for no one else can lay claim to the position of highest value in anyone's life.

As Louie Giglio put it, *"Worship is our response, both personal and corporate, to God for who He is and what He has done, expressed in the things we say and the way we live."*

Worship isn't merely something we do; it's an integral part of who we are as Christians.

Worship is our lifestyle. Worship means you are determining values; you are deciding what you desire the most. Worship means you're putting your priority in a right scene. Showing casing what is most important or what hold the first place in your life.

The truth is you become like the god you worship. This is established by the influence of worship the entire direction of your life is focus on.

Worship is a decision making about what your values are, what your priorities are and what you will eventually become.

Worship has a very huge weight on us from who is in you, to your priority and to whom you become.

A lukewarm heart cannot offer sincere worship, and a rebellious life cannot genuinely revere God. Worship should permeate every aspect of our lives.

TEN TRUTHS ABOUT WORSHIP

It's Not About Me: Worship is about God, not us. It goes beyond singing and emotional expressions; it involves adoring God with our lives and being in His presence.

Worship Style Is Contextual: Worship styles may differ depending on the setting, but as long as they align with the Word of God, they can be flexible and acceptable.

Style Preferences Can Change: Our worship style preferences can evolve as we grow and gain wisdom. Balancing hymns and praise choruses, for example, can be enriching.

The Word of God Is Central: True worship keeps the Word of God at its heart. Worship should never be limited to music; it should encompass the entire service.

Prayer Should Be Genuine: Meaningful, heartfelt, and passionate prayers are vital components of worship. Routine or insincere prayers may not lead to a worshipful encounter with God.

Worship Should Transform Lives: True worship should leave us changed. Encountering God in worship on Sunday should have a lasting impact on our lives throughout the week.

Worship Is Both Individual and Corporate: Worship extends beyond the Sunday service. It's a daily commitment and a lifestyle.

Corporate Worship Is a Gift: Gathering with fellow believers for corporate worship is a privilege that many around the world cherish, sometimes at great personal risk.

Authentic Living for Worship Leaders: Worship leaders should live lives consistent with the values they sing about. Authenticity is crucial for true worship.

True Worship Transforms: Worship that doesn't lead to positive change in people's lives cannot be considered true worship. It should edify and transform those who participate.

CHAPTER 2: WHY SHOULD WE WORSHIP GOD?

1 John 4:19 CEV says, *"We love because God loved us first."* *For His Love: God alone is worthy of our devotion, praise, and worship. He is God, our Creator, and we are commanded to praise and worship Him.*

Psalm 96:9 says, *"Worship the Lord in the splendor of His holiness; tremble before Him, all the earth."*

The answer to the title of this chapter is vital for our spiritual and physical well-being. However, when we are asked why we worship God, our answers are often vague because we tend to take worshiping God for granted without methodically thinking it through. The most basic answer is that He is the great and powerful Creator, and we, the insignificant and weak creation, therefore, humble ourselves and submit.

The more conscious we are of God's love for us, the less self-conscious we become. Love begins to shape the course of our lives, and worship becomes a natural outpouring of our transformed hearts.

"When you recognize God's awesomeness, it will evoke a certain response from you because you see something and

someone who is different and higher than you are. To worship is to act as an inferior before a superior." - JOSEPH L. GARLINGTON

WORSHIP AS A COMMANDMENT

A man once told me that he would never bow his knee to God, arguing, "What kind of father wants his own children to bow down to him?" He found it strange because he didn't want his children to bow down to him.

However, Philippians 2:9-10 says, "*Therefore God also has highly exalted Him and given Him the name which is above every name, that at the name of Jesus every knee should bow, of those in heaven, and of those on earth, and of those under the earth.*" Jesus is so exalted that eventually the knees of everyone, born or created, will bow in reverent homage to Him. This man was blinded to this truth.

Understanding the worship of God may seem simple, but practicing it is not always easy. Worship is simple only after we have learned some basic things about it. 1 Chronicles 16 largely consists of a psalm of praise and thanksgiving David composed to commemorate the bringing of the Ark of the Covenant to the Tabernacle in Jerusalem.

In verse 29, David writes, *"Give to the LORD the glory due His name; bring an offering, and come before Him. Oh, worship the LORD in the beauty of holiness!"*

Let us add to this Matthew 4:9-10, the occasion of Satan's third temptation of Christ in the wilderness. *"And he said to Him, 'All these things I will give You if You will fall down and worship me.' Then Jesus said to him, 'Away with you, Satan! For it is written, "You shall worship the LORD your God, and Him only you shall serve.'"*

Worship is a requirement for the Christian life, not something that can be brushed aside. We must place greater importance on this clear commandment from our Lord God.

WHERE AND WHEN SHOULD WE WORSHIP?

Ephesians 2:21 TLB says, *"We who believe are carefully joined with Christ as parts of a beautiful, constantly growing temple for God."*

The place where we have an encounter with the Lord becomes a very special place to us. Some may experience it in a church, on a mountain, during a vigil, etc. However, worship is more about relationship than a specific place.

That Samaritan woman talking with Jesus asked, "*'Sir, I can see that you are a prophet. Our father worshiped on this mountain, but you Jews claim that the place where we must worship is in Jerusalem." Jesus replied, "Believe me, woman, a time is coming when you will worship the Father neither on this mountain nor in Jerusalem... Yet a time is coming and now has come when the true worshipers will worship the* Father in spirit and truth, for they are the kind of worshipers the Father seeks." John 4:19-21, 23-24 says, *"God is spirit, and His worshipers must worship in spirit and in truth."*

First, notice that Jesus answered the "where" question by saying "in spirit and in truth." The believer's spirit is his essence, the very core of his being. The great commandment tells us to love the Lord with all our heart, soul, mind, and strength. The Holy Spirit lives inside each believer, and we can worship wherever we are, outside a church building as well as in one. Worship is not limited to a place because we live every moment in the presence of the Holy God.

Also, believers need to know that worship with other believers is essential. Hebrews 10:25 says, *"Not forsaking the assembling of ourselves together, as the manner of some is; but exhorting one another: and so much the more, as ye see the day approaching."*

WHEN SHOULD WE WORSHIP?

Christians should worship every time, every day, and live a life of worship, whether there is a gathering to meet others or not. Acts 17:28 tells us that we live and move and have our being in God. The Psalmist said there's nowhere we can go to get away from God - not into darkness, not across the ocean, not even into the depths of hell. Psalm 139:7-12 emphasizes God's omnipresence.

MY THOUGHTS ABOUT WORSHIP

If worship is about bringing pleasure to God, why wouldn't we want to worship? The Bible says in Psalms 34:1-2, "I *will praise the Lord at all times. His praise is always on my lips. My whole being praises the Lord.*" We don't have to be super spiritual to worship God continually. We can bring glory to God regardless of what we are doing as long as it honors Him.

Jesus told the Samaritan woman at the well, "*A time is coming, and it is already here! Even now the true worshipers are being led by the spirit to worship the Father according to the truth. These are the ones the Father is seeking to worship*

Him." John 4:23 CEV. Everyone born of the Spirit and truth is born to be a worshiper.

Worship is about exalting God with our entire life, not just through singing. It's not primarily about an experience, mood, or atmosphere. It's about making much of the authority, goodness, and holiness of God as seen in Jesus Christ. We can do that at any time, while eating, drinking, driving, studying, talking, working, or even playing.

Worship is an encounter with the living God. God's presence has always been a defining characteristic of God's people. As Christians, we should be keenly aware of God's promise to be with us and active among us. And we should long for the day when God will reveal Himself fully to us in heaven.

Worship in this life is only a foretaste of what is to come. While worship in the new heavens and new earth will certainly include singing, it will be much more.

BENEFITS OF WORSHIP

The purpose of worship is to get God into your environment and for His kingdom to be real in our lives. When God comes, speaks or moves, things change.

His presence will give us rest – (Ex. 33 v 14) Rest means comfort, quiet, settle down. To settle one's mind at rest.

God's presence brings peace: Like the account in the book of (Mark 4:35 – 40)

Jesus' presence brought peace "Quiet, Be still." God's presence in our life brings the same calm and peace when we worship Him

God's presence brings Joy (Ps. 16:11, Ps 84; 10). God's presence is the source of Joy. To experience more Joy in your life, spend more time with God.

When the Lord's presence is in a place with you, it makes you feel so good that you want to hang around for longer. You enjoy His presence so much that you find yourself doing things you normally can't do.

God's presence brings blessings (Psalm 65:4). The blessing of God is to receive or have anything and everything you need to fulfill your life's mandate.

God's presence is the answer to all the needs of our life.

God's presence brings wisdom and vision.

God's presence brings power.

CHAPTER 3: CALL TO WORSHIP

Genesis 22:2 presents one of the most enigmatic stories in the Bible regarding worship.

Abraham received a call to worship, but it was a shocking one. The God of love, whom I serve, who rescued me from a world filled with darkness, now commands me to take my only son and sacrifice him. In each of our lives, there exists a call to worship, much like that of Abraham.

Abraham stands as a prime example of faith in God. When we are filled with joy, we are most inclined to worship God.

Isaiah 63:7 says, *"I will extol the Lord's unfailing love; I will praise the Lord for all He has done. I will rejoice in His abundant goodness to Israel (to me), bestowed upon us through His mercy and love."*

I believe this was the sentiment in Abraham's heart as he journeyed to Mount Moriah, where God asked him to sacrifice his only son.

He could have chosen to murmur, but he opted to worship Elohim, rejoicing in his God. Worship transcends music, melody, or sweet voices; it is an encounter with God, a profound intimacy.

Worship is a path to the unknown mountain, a test of our faith.

Papa Abraham could have murmured, questioning God, but he chose to sing, *"Rejoice, rejoice and be glad in the Lord and rejoice, rejoice, be glad in the Lord and rejoice."*

Worship is indeed a journey to the mountain we don't know, a relationship of trust.

Note this: We don't worship to earn blessings or promotions; we worship to nurture our relationship with Him.

Worship is an offering, giving God all we have without holding back.

Worship is preparation; you can only worship the Father by yourself. You alone can find joy within yourself.

Worship is separation, being set apart for the Father alone.

Worship is obedience, as the Scripture says, "Rejoice, I say again, rejoice always."

Since worship involves sacrifice, it requires a broken spirit.

Abraham went to offer God only fire, wood, and a knife.

Fire - It consumes our past and purifies us.

 Isaiah 6:6, *"Then flew one of the seraphim unto me, having a live coal in his hand, which he had taken with the tongs from off the altar."*

Wood - It breaks the curse. Galatians 3:13, *"Christ hath redeemed us from the curse of the law, being made a curse for us: for it is written, cursed is every one that hangeth on a tree."*

Knife - It represents the shedding of blood. Hebrews 9:22, *"And almost all things are by the law purged with blood; and without shedding of blood is no remission."*

DEMANDS OF WORSHIP

Just as it was with Abraham, we, too, are called to worship. There are specific requirements when we answer God's call to worship.

First, we are called to a new place in Him. The Lord says, "Go to Moriah, to the place I will show you." God beckons us to new places in our walk with Him, responding to His call to worship in ways we've never done before.

Second, we are called to surrender to God's claims. The Lord said, "Sacrifice your only son." Just as Isaac was the fruit of Abraham and Sarah's bodies, there may be things in our lives more important to us than the call to worship, such as businesses, children, money, aspirations, or dreams. Worship demands total surrender, even of the things that seem most dear to us.

BLESSINGS OF WORSHIP

Just as Abraham's obedience to the call to worship led to a fresh revelation of God's nature and purpose, our response to the call to worship unveils a deeper understanding of God's character and His provision.

Abraham saw a new facet of God's nature and called the place Jehovah-Jireh - The Lord Will Provide. In our worship, we also uncover new aspects of God's nature. God calls us to worship not to exploit us, but to reveal and remove our fears. As we answer the call, we are introduced to the God who is our *"exceeding great reward."*

CHAPTER 4: WHO IS GOD?

Who is God? What is He like?

Six personality traits of God...

He is Knowable

God, who created the universe in all of its magnitude and creative details can be known by us. He tells us about Himself, but even goes beyond that. He welcomes us into a relationship, so that we personally can get to know Him. Not only can we know about Him, we can know Him intimately.

"Let not the wise man boast of his wisdom or the strong man boast of his strength or the rich man boast of his riches, but let him who boasts boast about this: that he understands and knows me, that I am the Lord, who exercises kindness, justice and righteousness on earth, for in these I delight," declares the Lord."* (Jeremiah 9:23 - 24)

He is Welcoming

God invites us to talk to Him and engage in what concerns us. We don't have to get our acts together first, neither do we need to be polite, theologically correct or holy. It is His nature to be loving and accepting when we go to Him.

"The Lord is near to all who call on Him, to all who call on Him in truth." (Psalms 145:18)

He is Creative

Everything we make is put together with existing materials or built on previous thoughts. God has the capacity of speaking things into existence, not just galaxies and life forms, but solutions to today's problems. God is creative and wants us to be aware of His power and rely on Him.

"Great is our Lord and mighty in power; His understanding has no limit." (Psalms 147:5)

"...Where does my help come from? My help comes from the Lord, the Maker of heaven and earth." (Psalms 121:1-2)

He is Forgiving

We sin. We tend to do things our way instead of God's way. And he sees and knows it. God does not merely overlook such sin, but is prepared to judge and condemn people for their sin. However, God is forgiving and will forgive us from the moment we begin a relationship with Him. Jesus, the Son of God, paid for our sin with His death on a cross. He rose from the dead and offers us this forgiveness.

"We are made right in God's sight when we trust in Jesus Christ to take away our sins. And we all can be saved in this same way, no matter who we are or what we have done... We are made right with God when we believe that Jesus shed his blood, sacrificing his life for us." (Romans 3:22,25)

He is Honest

Just like a person who lets you know their thoughts and feelings, God clearly tells us about Himself, the possible difference being, He is always honest. Everything He says about Himself, or about us, is reliable information. Truer than our feelings, thoughts, and perception, God is totally accurate and honest in what He says. Every promise He makes to us can be fully counted on; He means it. We can take Him for His word.

"The unfolding of your words gives light; it gives understanding to the simple. Your word is a lamp to my feet and a light to my path." (Psalms 119:130,105)

He is Capable

How would you like to be always 100% right, about everything? God is. His wisdom is unlimited. He understands all the elements of a situation, including the history and future events related to it. We do not have to update Him, counsel or persuade Him to do the right thing. He will, because He is capable and His motives are pure. If we trust Him, He will never make a mistake, never undercut or deceive us. He can be fully trusted to do what is right, in all circumstances, at all times.

"No one whose hope is in you will ever be put to shame..." (Psalms 25:3)

God is ELOHIM - Our creator

Elohim is one of the three divine names by which the Creator is known. The creation account is probably the most difficult and most enigmatic passages in the Bible. It starts at the beginning and it doesn't really end.

There are three stages upon which creation unfolds. The first stage stretches from Genesis 1:1 to 2:4. During this period God is known as Elohim. From Genesis 2:4 He is known as YHWH Elohim. The third stage starts around the Noah cycle and flows over into the Abraham cycle and beyond across the rest of the Bible. Abraham, after all, was the first to believe and became not only a new creation but also the first of a new continuum of new creations. During this stage, God is known as Dabar YHWH, or Word Of God.

When used to refer to the true God, "Elohim" denotes what is called by linguists a plural of majesty, honour, or fullness. That is, He is GOD in the fullest sense of the word. He is "GOD of gods" or literally, "ELOHIM of *elohims*" (Deut. 10:17; Psalma 136:2).

In the Greek translation of the Hebrew Bible (the Septuagint), where Elohim refers to the true God, the singular theos is used.

Genesis 1:1 Hebrew — *"In the beginning, Elohim created the heavens and the earth."*
Genesis 1:1 Greek — *"In the beginning, Theos made the heavens and the earth."*

In the Hebrew Bible, there are four words translated "God": El, Elah, Elo'ah, Elohim.

The oldest Semitic word meaning "God" is El. Linguists believe its base meaning is strength or power. "El" is the Strong One, or the Deity (God). It appears 238x in the Bible, and is first used in Genesis 14:18 in the phrase "God Most High" [El Elyon].

The Canaanites called their chief deity *El, the Mighty Bull.* After the Israelites entered Canaan, they adopted this generic word "El" for their God, though "Elohim" took precedence. In some Canaanite myths, one of El's sons was the notorious Ba'al, the nemesis of the true God throughout much of Israel's history.

In the Bible, El is often combined in proper names: Isra-El; Shmu-El (Samuel); El-ijah; Immanu-El; Jo-El; Dani-El; Beth-El. It's also found in compounds: El Shaddai, El Elyon, El Roi, ElOlam.

Elah is the Aramaic word for "God" used in the Aramaic portions of Daniel and Ezra and one verse in Jeremiah (10:11). Its plural form Elahin is used at least once for the true God (Dan. 5:23).

ELOHIM THE CREATOR

The word Elo'ah is used some 57 times, mostly in the book of Job. It is likely the singular form behind Elohim.

The generic term Elohim refers to the true "God" (2507x), as well as to "gods," "goddesses," and things divine or mighty. In total, it occurs 2602 times in the HB.

The first thing to note is that the phenomenon of pluralizing certain nouns is common in the Bible. Thus, the plural Elohim should be interpreted in light of these language patterns. Here is a summary of what these patterns and realities reveal.

Biblical usage suggests that Elohim reflects a "plural of honor" or "plural of fulness." The plural ending gives greater honor to God. It's like capitalizing the word, instead of printing "god." Or it's analogous to printing GOD or GOD, though Hebrew has no capital and small letters.

"GOD is the Greatest God of all."

The first of the Ten Commandments says, "I am YHVH your Elohim . . . you shall have no other elohim in my presence" (Exo. 20:2-3). Should "other elohim" be

The Only or True Elohim

rendered "other gods" or "other God"? The ambiguity is likely intended. Moses says God is "GOD of gods" or literally, "Elohim of elohims" (Deut. 10:17).

The Lord of Lords

The pluralizing impulse extends beyond Elohim. Typically, when God is called "Lord" or "Master" (Adon) the word usually occurs as a plural: Adonim or Adonai. As with Elohim, God is LORD in the fullest sense of the word: Master of all.

As Deuteronomy 10:17 tells us, Elohim is supreme over all elohims, it also says He is "Lord of lords: Adonim of adonims" — whether the lords are divine or human.

God can also be known as: Holy One (kedoshim), Teacher (morim), Maker (osim), Husband (baalim), Most High (elyonin, Aramaic).

The messianic king *may* be called Elohim in Psalm 45:6: *"Your throne, O Elohim, is forever and ever."* But the Hebrew can be translated as: *"Your throne is Elohim forever and ever."*

Isaiah uses the ancient word El in two messianic titles: Immanu-El ("with us is El"; 7:14, 8:8) and El Gibbor ("El is a warrior" or a "Divine warrior", 9:5).

CHAPTER 5: THE SECRET PLACE

Psalm 91:1-2 says, *"He who dwells in the secret place of the Most High shall abide under the shadow of the Almighty. I will say of the Lord, 'He is my refuge and my fortress; my God, in Him I will trust.'"*

The term **"SECRET PLACE"** appears in both the Old and New Testaments several times. It can be described as a **"SHELTER,"** **"COVERING,"** or **"DWELLING."**

The concept of the secret place originates from the Hebrew word **"CETHER,"** meaning **"TO HIDE"** or be concealed.

In Psalm 139:15, *it speaks of the hidden world of a mother's womb as a child develops, emphasizing the secrecy and protection of this place.*

Psalm 27:5 *conveys that in times of trouble, God conceals us in His tabernacle, providing a state of peace in the midst of trials and attacks.*

The **"SECRET PLACE"** is:

A place of peace, as Jesus stated in John 16:33, *"In the world you will have tribulation, but in Me, you will have peace."*

A place of brightness, where there cannot be a shadow without light, as mentioned in Psalm 91:1.

A place of power, enabling us to be fruitful, as described in John 15:1.

A place of revelation, where time spent in God's presence unveils our true thoughts and selfish motivations, as illustrated in Isaiah 6:1-5.

A place of growth, where the fruit of the Spirit takes root, shifting our perspective from earthly frustrations to eternal significance.

The concept of a secret place originates with God, who is a Spirit, and whose glory is beyond human perception or comprehension. Therefore, we must seek Him in the secret places of our hearts to commune with Him.

In Exodus 33:20-22, when Moses desired to see the glory of God, the Lord explained that no one could see God and live. So, God allowed Moses to see His glory from a 'secret place' in a cleft in the rock, emphasizing that God's presence can only be enjoyed when we enter His secret place.

Let me share a personal experience of the secret place.

Years ago my son fell terribly ill, we took him to the hospital and we were asked to run several medical test. After it was carried out, the diagnosis was Colonic volvulus (intestinal twisting). I argued with the doctor that my son eats well and he is healthy and such can not happen.

In that moment, his stomach had swollen, eyes turned pale and closed. When I realized this, I rushed out of the room to a silent place in the hospital and worshipped God. I asked Him what was going on and what we need to do.

At this time I was told to sign an undertaking for the surgery process to commence. I kept mute but what I remember vividly were songs registered in my heart that kept flowing from my lips.

Immediately I heard repair and restore. A scriptural light came directly to my heart.

Then they gave it to the workmen who were appointed over the house of the LORD, and the workmen who were working in the house of the LORD gave it [to others] to repair and restore the house (temple).

2 Chronicles 34:10 (Amplified)

By faith I rejoiced as he was moved to the theatre for the procession, my worship got more intense. The good news is, I already saw the end of the operation before it started.

Hallelujah!

Today, my boy is very sound and healthy to the glory of God.

Pay attention to this!

The secret place is where we grow in our relationship and communion with God, as he reveals his heart and mind to us. It is a place of power, shield, and protection.

It is a place of insight and revelation where the Father, Son and The Holy-Spirit reveals the secret of the season for your life.

BENEFITS OF THE SECRET PLACE

In the secret place, God keeps us safe and watches over us, as described in Psalm 32:7, *"You are my hiding place, You shall preserve me from trouble, You shall surround me with songs of deliverance."*

There is deliverance in the secret place, freeing us from our past and the accusations of others, as depicted in Psalm 91:3-7.

The secret place provides divine protection, ensuring that no weapon formed against us shall prosper and every tongue that rises against us in judgment shall be condemned, as seen in Psalm 91:7-10.

In the secret place, God offers divine guidance, just as in the story of Elijah where God provided supply, attention, and prosperity, as revealed in verses 4 and 14.

The secret place is a constant place of worship, often serving as a personal devotion or quiet time where spiritual exchange and communication happen.

CHAPTER 6: INTIMACY WITH GOD

"One thing have I desired of the Lord, that will I seek after; that I may dwell in the house of the Lord all the days of my life, to behold the beauty of the Lord, and to inquire in His temple." (Psalm 27:4)

Let's briefly discuss Incense, Altar, and the Temple in the context of contemporary worship in truth and in spirit.

There exists a spiritual connection between our worship experiences with the Lord and how the priests of Solomon's Temple worshipped Him. There is a valid Scriptural comparison between true worshippers of God who "worship the Lord in Spirit and Truth" (John 4:23) and the priests who worshipped the Lord "in the beauty of holiness" at the Incense Altar.

Though the latter was under the Old Covenant, with Christ, the comparison holds, and Scripture underscores its importance (2 Cor. 6:16, 1 Cor. 3:16).

The order of service for the priests was as follows:

When the priests first entered the Inner Court, they immediately went to the Bronze Lavers, where they washed their hands and feet. Then, they approached the Brazen Altar, where they sacrificed animals to cleanse the sins of the people. Next, they immersed themselves in the Molten Sea.

Finally, they took a censer filled with hot coals from the Brazen Altar, entered the temple, changed their clothes, and proceeded to the Holy Place. In the Holy Place, they took incense, sprinkled it over the coals on the Golden Incense Altar, removed their shoes, prostrated themselves, and worshiped the Lord in the "beauty of holiness" (Exodus 25:22).

To me, this worship service serves as a model for how the Lord wants us to deal with our sin, be reconciled to Him, and enter His presence. The Bronze Lavers, the Brazen Altar, and the Molten Sea represent the three cleansing steps God has provided in Scripture to purify ourselves from "all filthiness of [our] flesh and spirit" (2 Corinthians 7:1) and enable us to approach Him:

 (1) Confess and repent of our sin and self;

(2) Surrender these things to Him; and finally,

(3) Immerse ourselves in His Word to replace falsehoods with His truth.

ONENESS WITH THE LORD

Our natural strength is addressed on the Brazen Altar (in the Inner Court), but it is not until we reach the Incense Altar (in the Holy Place) that we experience genuine oneness, communion, and intimacy with Him. Our spirit is now fortified to freely guide our soul in all things. This is how God intended us to live from the beginning. The Incense Altar symbolizes the complete union of our spirit with His Spirit.

God desires us to be "one" with Him, not only positionally (which occurs at our new birth) but also experientially (in our daily walk), even if it starts with just a few moments a day. Perhaps the following day, we can stay in this communion for a longer period, and the day after, even longer still. Only Jesus was able to maintain this perfect experiential communion with the Father continually because He was sinless.

Experiential union with Christ, that deeper merging of our spirits, represents the pinnacle of our relationship with Him. This is the fulfillment, the perfection, and the "fullness of God" that Scripture speaks of and that He has designed for each one of us. Everything on the inside and outside becomes His!

The Incense Altar, once again, symbolizes this experiential union of our spirits. However, just as the perfume from the Incense Altar retained its own unique properties as it rose from the altar (though it was united with the cloud of fire), we retain our individuality and humanity when we become experientially united with God.

An analogy that might aid in understanding this paradox is that the Incense Altar was located just outside the veil to the Holy of Holies. But when reading Scripture, it seems as if the Incense Altar was considered part of the Holy of Holies.

 Read Leviticus 16:12-13, *"And he shall take a censer full of burning coals of fire from off the altar before the Lord, and his hands full of sweet incense beaten small, and bring it within the veil: And he shall put the incense upon the fire before the Lord, that the cloud of the incense may cover the mercy seat that is upon the testimony..."*

Similarly, we are considered to be positionally one with the Lord due to our new birth; however, experientially, it's often a different story.

OFFERING OF THE INCENSE

Incense means "to blow or to breathe."

Throughout Scripture, incense is referred to as "sweet smoke." It symbolizes our praise, prayers, and worship. Incense and the Golden Altar were consistently associated with the Temple and its worship services. For instance, Revelation 8:3-4 tells us, *"And another angel came and stood at the altar, having a golden censer; and there was given unto him much incense, that he should offer it with the prayers of all saints upon the golden altar which was before the throne. And the smoke of the incense, which came with the prayers of the saints, ascended up before God..."* (See also Psalm 141:2).

Taking that hot piece of coal from the Brazen Altar (symbolic of our crucified life), placing it on the Incense Altar, and witnessing the perfume and fire becoming one, beautifully depicts what it means to worship Him. As we offer God the incense of our fully surrendered lives, we become "one," just as the fire and wood do.

Incense represents the fragrance of our lives. A foul scent signifies an impure or unholy life, while a pleasant one signifies a holy or pure life. When sin and self no longer form a barrier to our approach to God, a sweet aroma can rise before Him. In other words, as we become "one" with Him, we emit the fragrance of His Life.

That incense, the sweet fragrance of holiness, ascends to God as an acceptable offering. It's the result of our sanctification and purification. 2 Corinthians 2:15 tells us that *"We are unto God a sweet savor of Christ."* This sweet fragrance "before the Lord" assures us access to His throne

Malachi 1:11 prophesies that in the end times, His name shall be great among the Gentiles, and in every place, incense shall be offered unto His name. In other words, in these end times, God desires all Christians everywhere and in every place to offer incense (worship) to His name.

CHAPTER 7: TRAITS OF A WORSHIPPER

"Let us draw near with a true heart in full assurance of faith, having our hearts sprinkled from an evil conscience and our bodies washed with pure water." Hebrews 10:22

A worshipper is a call out. someone who is of faith because they have built an intimate relationship with God and have come to know His attributes.

Every human being is a worshipper. We crave to worship one thing or the other. We could see the example of the Isrealist worshipping Image made by them.

The difference between our worship and the worship of the world is that **we worship Eternal God** – The only **one that is worthy**. The Object of our worship is the invisible, personal, omnipotent, omnipresent, omniscient, immutable God. We express our affections for a God that would give Himself for His people. We serve and obey a God that created the heavens and the earth.

God wants worshipers to have a sincere heart, zero hypocrisy or religious acts. He wants sincere and loyal hearts.

Obedience to God is a core value of a worshiper. Yielding and taking the word of God as it is.

In Psalm 149:4. For the Lord takes pleasure in his people; he adorns the humble with salvation. Every worshipper of King of Glory have to possess the spirit of humility. Humility in God's sight requires a heart-driven attitude of meekness. A humble person seek and do all according to the leading of the Lord.

Prayer is an act of communicating and seeking the will of the father. A worshipper must be Prayerful person. Knowing the heart of the father is through hot felt and consistence prayer. - Worshippers are prayerful.

Dedication is writing your name on the bottom of a blank sheet of paper and handling it to the Lord for Him to fill in -

Author: Rick Renner

Dedication is getting out of your will for His will to take place. Worshippers are dedicated. Must be a true representative of the father.

"For if we live, we live to the Lord, and if we die, we die to the Lord. So then, whether we live or whether we die, we are the Lord's." Romans 14:8

Colossians 3 17 says And whatever you do, in word or deed, do everything in the name of the Lord Jesus, giving thanks to God the Father through him. That is the life of a worshipper.

Submissiveness - Worshippers are submissive. Dictionary meaning for submissive says inclined or ready to submit or yield to the authority of another; unresistingly or humbly obedient:

Submissive is total yield unto the Lord. The word submission comes from the word 'hupotasso' which speaks of a soldier under the military command of an officer. It was also used to mean 'to subordinate, to subject, to subject one's self, obey, to submit to one's control, to yield to one's admonition or advice, to obey, be subject.' Someone has remarked that 'it was "a voluntary attitude of giving in, cooperating, assuming responsibility, and carrying a burden".

1 Corinthians 11:24 "And when he had given thanks, he brake it, and said, Take, eat: this is my body, which is broken for you: this do in remembrance of me". Brokenness is a character of a worshipper. Jesus did not cut the bread. He broke it. He was painting a picture of what was about to happen to His body. Worshipper are the body of Christ. God beautify our life when we are broken. Brokenness is a condition during which God allows circumstances to control our lives to the point that we must totally depend on him.

Brokenness is a state of mind, whereby we recognize our personal weaknesses and limitations before God, and surrender to his will.

Spiritual sensitivity - According to the Dictionary of Bible Themes, *"Spiritual sensitivity is the ability to perceive and respond to the call of God or the spiritual demands of the moment."* It adds that over-sensitivity and lack of sensitivity are extremes to be avoided. Every child of God needs to develop or cultivate spiritual sensitivity. It's not automatic because someone is born again.

Spiritual sensitivity is the ability to understand the voice of God through your spirit man. It is a sign you have encountered the wisdom of God and have the ability to discern spiritual issues like where to go and the direction to follow without relying on your five senses.

Worshipers feed and drink from his spiritual source. Worshiper are meant to be lead by the Spirit of the Lord and when we follow Him wholehearted.

LOOKING UNTO JESUS

The question is as a worshiper where do you look unto for supplies?

A life that lacks direction has lost its vibes, if we keep doing things the same way and expect to have a result that is a sign of insanity. John F. Kennedy said efforts and courage are not enough without purpose and direction.

If you have no good drive in you, your life will not be steered through a good direction. It will miss its destined station. Passion or drive is what moves the vehicle of a fulfilled life. - Israel Moore.

"Looking unto Jesus the author and the finisher of our faith." I like how amplified bible put it.

 "Looking away {from all that will detract} to Jesus who is the leader and the source of our faith { giving the first incentive for our belief} and is also its finisher} {bringing it to maturity and perfection} he for the joy {of obtaining the prize} that was set before him, endured the cross despising and ignoring the shame, and is now seated at the right hand of the throne of God.

{Psalm 110vs1}- The Lord {God} says to my Lord {the Messiah} sit at My right hand, until I make Your adversaries {your enemy} footstool.

_ To ''look'' is to be 'focused', directing one's gaze in a specified direction.

_ To direct your eyes in order to see with your mind.

_ One can see and may not look.

_ looking unto Jesus means, if you are drowning and somebody walk pass you, you do not look at him, you look unto Him.

-is relying on Jesus rather than solely on the actions or behavior of others.

Looking unto Jesus as the Author and Finisher of our faith, is finding strength, guidance, and endurance in Him to navigate the complexities of the spiritual journey and grow in relationship with God.

There are many obstacles, challenges difficulties that may comes our ways, just to distract us from whom we are meant to be. Sometimes they test of our times. It could be either disagreement in our relationship that may cause a major brake up. Sickness that collapse the family finances. One adorable child turn to be the black sheep of the house.

Behold, the Lord's eye is upon those who fear Him [who revere and worship Him with awe], who wait for Him and hope in His mercy and loving-kindness, Psalm 33:18 AMP CE

_ When you look unto Him, you are turning to Him and expecting Him to rescue you.

Be encourage to keep your focus, looking at Jesus

Therefore then, since we are surrounded by so great a cloud of witnesses [who have borne testimony to the Truth], let us strip off and throw aside every encumbrance (unnecessary weight) and that sin which so readily (deftly and cleverly) clings to and entangles us, and let us run with patient endurance and steady and active persistence the appointed course of the race that is set before us, Hebrews 12:1

Amplified Bible, Classic Edition

_We are called to look unto Jesus who is our perfect example of faith.

Because He is the author and the finisher of our faith. His example in the race of life has none comparable to it.

Jesus scorned the shame on the cross, since he knows where he is coming from and where he is going.

He did not allow anything to hinder Him from attaining His goal of sitting at the right hand of the throne of God.

Life is a "race'' just like an athlete in the stadium.

Jesus was disciplined in knowing and doing the will of His Father {Luke 22vs42}- saying Father, if thou be willing, remove this cup from Me, nevertheless not My will but Thine be done.

He endured and persevered to the end of His goal and now become for us unbeatable example and a point of focus.

Look unto Jesus and win the race; it demands avoidant of all unnecessary weight. What load of life are you carrying? {Galatians 5vs20-21}

The rules should be observed. {1st Corinthians 9vs26]- *"I therefore so run, not as uncertainly; so fight I, not as one that beats the air."*

In a place of worship our focus is being renew. Our intention is been sharpened to what we are born to be.

Worship open the eye of our understanding to behold the author and the finisher of our life.

<u>A worshiper's life is meant to consecrated</u>

Spirit, soul, and body belong to the Lord only. 1 Thessalonians 5vs23 - *And the very God of prove sanctify you wholly, and I pray God your whole spirit and soul and boy be preserved blameless unto the coming of our lord Jesus Christ. SPIRIT- part of you that connect with God, the real you.*

SOUL - Your mind, will and emotion

Fix your eyes on Him [Hebrew 126vs2]/Job 35vs5 – *"Look unto the heavens and see, and behold the cloud which are higher than thou."*

Let your feet walk in His way. [Hebrew 12vs1, Genesis 5vs22] *Then Enoch walked with God three hundred years after he became the father of Methuselah. [Genesis 5vs24 - Enoch walked with God and he was not, for God took him.* To walk with God also imply to fellowship with God; walk with God spiritually.

Let your hand always be ready to do good. [Ephesians 4vs28]. Let your thought be busy. Meditate on the things of God. Colossians 3vs2 - Set you affection on things above, not on things on the earth.

Let your heart be confirmed by grace. [Hebrew 13vs9].

Let your body be a living sacrifice - Rom. 12:1, *"I beseech you therefore, brethren, by the mercies of God, that ye present your bodies a living sacrifice, holy, acceptable unto God, which is your reasonable service."*

Lev. 20:2, *"Tell the Israelites: If Israelites or foreigners living among you give one of their children as a sacrifice to the god Molech, they must be put to death. The common people must stone them to death."*

1Pet. 2:5, *"Ye also, as lively stones, are built up a spiritual house, an holy priesthood, to offer up spiritual sacrifices, acceptable to God by Jesus Christ."*

WHEN YOU LOOK UNTO JESUS

You have salvation from sin. [John 1vs29].

You love him more. [2 Corinthians 5vs14-16]

You Commune with Jesus [Ephesians 5vs1-2]

You are separated from the world. [Galatians 1vs4]

You are encouraged to follow Jesus, thereby being a good example to others. [1 Peter 2vs21-24]

You are healed. [Psalm 34vs5]

Strength in tribulation [Hebrew 12vs3].

QUOTES ON WORSHIP

"The whole person, with all his senses, with both mind and body, needs to be involved in genuine worship." - Jerry Kerns

"The most valuable thing the Psalms do for me is to express the same delight in God which made David dance." - C.S. Lewis

"When God's people begin to praise and worship Him using the Biblical methods He gives, the Power of His presence comes among His people in an even greater measure." - Graham Truscott

"God is to be praised with the voice, and the heart should go therewith in holy exultation." - Charles H. Spurgeon

"Worship is an it-is-well-with-my-soul experience." - Robert Webber

"Without worship, we go about miserable." - A. W. Tozer

"'A glimpse of God will save you. To gaze at Him will sanctify you." - Manley Beasley

"We only learn to behave ourselves in the presence of God." - C. S. Lewis

"Worship is the real you"

"Worship is your lifestyle.

The Ministry of the Shofar

The Shofar - The ram's horn trumpet, is one of the ancient wind instruments played by the ancient Israelites.

The Shofar is exceedingly loud and when it sounded from the thick cloud on Sinai it made all in the camp tremble

While other musical instruments were in each age constructed according to the most advanced contemporary practice, the trumpet family being represented by the long straight silver "hazozerah", the Shofar has never varied in structure from its prehistoric simplicity and crudity.

The curved Shofar is symbolic of the contrite heart repenting on the most solemn day of Rosh ha shanah and Yom kip pur.

The "Shofar" represents the spokesmen of Yahweh the Almighty God of Israel; through whom His Spirit declares the truth. It is a musical instrument of antiquity - "of God's own making".

The Shofar is also a mighty instrument of praise and worship.

Throughout time it has been used by people to breakthrough great obstacles, defeat powerful enemies, and open the way for awesome demonstrations of the power and presence of God.

The Shofar, though is a natural instrument, is also a supernatural one. It is the only instrument God Himself sounds to release justice over darkness and establish righteousness over the earth and affairs of people.

The Shofar is an instrument for today's victory.

Scriptural background of Shofar

"3 When both horns sound, all the people will gather in front of you at the door of the meeting tent. 4 If only one horn sounds, then the leaders, the heads of the families of Israel,

will gather in front of you. 5 When you blow the horn to tell of danger, the people whose tents are on the east side will leave. 6 When you blow the horn to tell of danger a second time, the people whose tents are on the south side will leave. A horn telling of danger will be blown when they are to move on. 7 But when the people are to be gathered together, you will blow the horn without the sound of danger. 8 Aaron's sons, the religious leaders, will blow the horns. This will be a Law for all your people forever. 9 When you go to war in your land against those who fight you, then sound the horns to tell of war. That way you will be remembered before the Lord your God, and be saved from those who hate you.." Numbers 10:3-*9* New Life Version

"On the morning of the third day there was thunder and lightning. A cloud covered the mountain, and a very loud horn sounded. All the people among the tents shook with fear. 17 Then Moses brought the people from among the tents to meet God. They stood at the base of the mountain. 18 Mount Sinai was all in smoke because the Lord came down upon it in fire. Its smoke went up like the smoke of a stove. And the whole mountain shook. 19 The sound of the horn became louder and louder. Moses spoke, and God

answered him with thunder..” *Exodus 19:16-19* New Life Version

WHO CAN BLOW THE SHOFAR

1) Angels blow the Shofar

“He will send His angels with the loud sound of a horn. They will gather God's people together from the four winds. They will come from one end of the heavens to the other..” Matt. 24:31

2) The Priests blow the Shofar

“Aaron's sons, the religious leaders, will blow the horns. This will be a Law for all your people forever..” Numbers 10:8

WHO ARE THE PRIESTS?

1Pet. 2:9, *“But ye are a chosen generation, a royal priesthood, an holy nation, a peculiar people; that ye should shew forth the praises of him who hath called you out of darkness into his marvelous light.”*

All believing Christians are priests

When the Shofar is blown the devil is confused.

What is Special about the sound of the Shofar

"I was under the Spirit's power on the Lord's Day when I heard a loud voice behind me like the loud sound of a horn." Revelation 1:10

"After this, I looked and saw a door standing open in heaven. The first voice I heard was like the loud sound of a horn. It said, "Come up here. I will show you what must happen after these things.." Revelation 4:1

The voice of God is like the sound of a Shofar

"Wherein in time past ye walked according to the course of this world, according to the prince of the power of the air, the spirit that now worketh in the children of disobedience." Eph 2:2

The devil is the prince and power of the air.

When the shofar is blown, we release power of God into the air (the devil's camp).

The sound of the Shofar (trumpet) is like the voice of God.

Each time we sound it, we are hammering and destroying the enemy's camp with the voice of God.

Generally, when I blow it, I notice the atmosphere of the room or the gathering change.

"In the beginning God created the heaven and the earth. And the earth was without form, and void; and darkness was upon the face of the deep. And the Spirit of God moved upon the face of the waters. And God said, Let there be light: and there was light." Gen 1:1-3

When we blow a Shofar, we are releasing the voice of God. We are releasing God's power, Jehovah Elohim and anointing into the atmosphere to a specific purpose. It can be for healing, for deliverance, for protection and also to stop any evil force that want to dominate the atmosphere.

What is Expected to Happen When the Shofar is Sounded/Blown.

Sickness is of the enemy and he uses to oppress people. When we blow the Shofar in obedience to the ordinance, God delivers people from the enemies that oppress them (Pain, sickness, lack).

When the Shofar is blown, the enemy's camp goes into confusion and they turn on each other with the sword.

Some years back in the area I stayed. The traditionalist make an announcement that there will no movement from 11pm till 6am that they want to do there ritual (Oro day) and that they will enter each streets. I came out that evening and blow the shofar. At night they started going from street to street doing there shants. When they entered my street just about some houses to mine it just started raining and they all scattered and ran away.

man next to him among the tents. And the army ran away as far as Beth-shittah toward Zererah. They went as far as the land of Abel-meholah, by Tabbath." Judges 7:21

The sound of the Shofar with the shout of the people of God brought down the walls of Jericho.

"So the people called out and the religious leaders blew the horns. When the people heard the sound of the horns, they called out even louder. And the wall fell to the ground. All the people went straight in and took the city." Joshua 6:20

OBEDIENCE is the key word to receive exactly what God promised,

The Shofar blast is a commandment - a divine decree that connects its earthly observer with its supernatural commander.

Its sound announces the year of Jubilee, year of abundance, year of financial and all-round increase.

"On the days you are glad and at the time of your special suppers and on the first days of your months, blow the horns.

Blow the horns over your burnt gifts and over your peace gifts. Then you will be remembered before your God. I am the Lord your God." Numbers 10:10

"God is gone up with a shout, the LORD with the sound of (Shofar) trumpet." Psalm 47:5

The Shofar is an instrument of worship

"With trumpets and sound of cornet make a joyful noise before the LORD, the King." Psalms 98:6

"Praise him with the sound of the trumpet: praise him with the psaltery and harp." Psalms 150:3

Is a trumpet of the jubilee - proclaiming Liberty

"9 Then let the horn be heard on the tenth day of the seventh month. On the day to be made free from sin you will let a horn be heard all through your land. 10 You will honor the fiftieth year as holy. And let it be known in all the land that all who are living there are free. It will be a happy time for you. Each of you will return to what is his. Each will return to his family..” *Leveticus 25:9-10*

The Shofar is blown to remind God of His provision

"And Abraham lifted up his eyes, and looked, and behold behind him a ram caught in a thicket by his horns: and Abraham went and took the ram, and offered him up for a burnt offering in the stead of his son." Genesis 22:1-3

"Then I brought up the princes of Judah upon the wall, and appointed two great companies of them that gave thanks, whereof one went on the right hand upon the wall toward the dung gate: And after them went Hoshaiah, and half of the princes of Judah, And Azariah, Ezra, and Meshullam, Judah, and Benjamin, and Shemaiah, and Jeremiah. And certain of the priests' sons with trumpets; namely, Zechariah the son of Jonathan, the son of Shemaiah, the son of Mattaniah, the son of Michaiah, the son of Zaccur, the son of Asaph." Neh 12:31-35

To stop Battle

"Then Abner looked behind him, and said, Art thou Asahel? And he answered, I am." 2Sam 2:20

Return of the Ark

"So David and all the house of Israel brought up the ark of the LORD with shouting, and with the sound of the trumpet." *2Sam 6:15*

The Lord shall blow the Shofar

"Then the Lord will be seen over them, and His arrow will go out like lightning. The Lord God will blow the horn and go in the storm winds of the south.." Zechariah 9:14,

"All you people of the world, you who live on the earth, as soon as a flag is raised on the mountain, you will see it. As soon as the horn is sounded, you will hear it." Isaiah 18:3

"In that day a great horn will be blown. Those who were dying in the land of Assyria and those who were sent everywhere through the land of Egypt will come and worship the Lord on the holy mountain at Jerusalem." Isaiah 27:13

God is calling some to blow the Shofar and He is calling all to be human Shofars, the carriers of God's Power and anointing, to cry aloud, to lift up our voice, to let a dying world know about Jesus.

Announcement of God's presence

"So David and all those of the family of Israel were bringing (the ark) the special box of the Lord with a loud voice and the sound of the horn." 2Sam 6:15

Blowing the shofar is not for entertainment, is an Apostolic and Prophetic direction of God,

 "But the Spirit of the Lord came upon Gideon. He blew a horn and called together the Abiezerites to follow him." Judges 6:34

TESTIMONIALS OF THE SHOFAR

Ministering with the Shofar is so powerful. In that moment you are strategically God's battle axe, connected to his voice.

I was invited to a worship meeting where I ministered.

Surprisingly after the Shofar was blown, my attention was called to an instant testimony of a lady from a hair salon not far from the Church, matter of fact she came to the worship center with her hair, half way done.

According to her, the sound of the shofar was loud in her ears and a voice repeatedly spoke audibly saying " I have called you to serve". With tears in her eyes - seeing that she turned her back against God due to some experiences but now restored.

Is it not miraculous to witness the mighty hand of God?

In other words, Shofar is a means to call for restitution with God, no matter how much you've messed up or gone astray, God's love is strategically revealed through this instrument for a wake up call.

Another importance of the Shofar is the healing and deliverance it brings to God's people.

The experience I had at a different worship meeting where I ministered, till present it remains amazing to me.

I heard this testimony from the convener after I had left. A lady got healed on her way home from partial deafness, infact she was scheduled for a surgery to flush out the wax in her ear. As God had his way, her ear popped open.

Hallelujah!

The interesting part is, I had left the meeting for the car park ready to leave, then I received a prompt from the holy spirit not to leave that auditorium and I obeyed immediately.

Unknowingly to me, the minister on stage was led to invite me to blow the shofar once more. It was after this, testimonies started to roll in.

Why did I share those practical examples?

The reason is simply because God's intention to heal and deliver us in this present time is as real as it was millions of years ago.

The Spirit of the Lord prepares the people of God for the miraculous. When the Spirit moved upon Gideon and after he blew the Shofar the result was marvelous.

The sound of the Shofar signifies all that is dear to the God of Israel who I call Jehovah Elohim.

The Shofar sounds brings truth, repentance, obedience, dedication, restoration, sanctification, warning, expectation victory and resurrection from the dead.

About the Author

EWULOTAN AYODEJI PETER is a seasoned teacher of the word, bringing a profound gift of administration to his ministry. A psalmist and the visionary convener of Switch Worship Ministry (Switch-to-Worship), he serves as the Lead Pastor of ELOHIM FAMILY SANCTUARY in Lagos, Nigeria.

A graduate of Lagos State University with a BSc in Accounting. His passion for organizing live programs and events led him to become a certified Scrum Master and Program Director at New Leaf Radio and country Director of New Leaf Foundation. He is a dynamic public speaker and a sought-after facilitator at Church Growth seminars.

Dr. Pst. Deji holds a PHD from International Institute for Church Growth, Church Management Consult. Growth Bible College.

His dedication to empowering lives extends to counseling, where he earned credentials from TIMFA (The Institute for Marriage and Family Affairs) and ADI COLLEGE OF COUNSELLING AND PSYCHOTHERAPY, being a proud member of ANEPCO (AFRICA NETWORK OF PROFESSIONAL COUNSELLORS).

As a mindset change leader and professional counselor, he specializes in pre-marital counseling, couples conflict management, and grief therapy. He serves as the Director of REUEL Counselor.